THE HOSPITAL BOOK

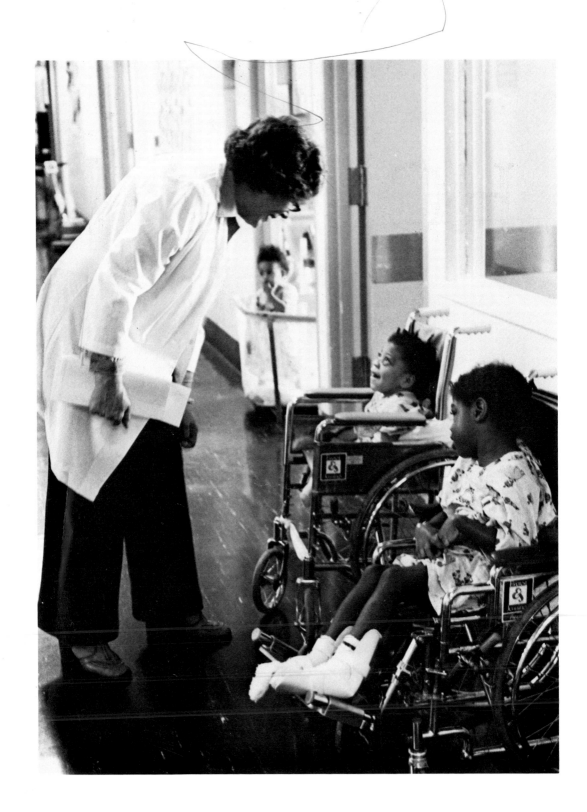

THE HOSPITAL BOOK

TEXT BY

James Howe

PHOTOGRAPHS BY

Mal Warshaw

MORROW JUNIOR BOOKS · NEW YORK

Originally published in 1981 by Crown Publishers, Inc., in a slightly different format.

Printed in the United States of America.

    2   3   4   5   6   7   8   9   10

Library of Congress Cataloging-in-Publication Data
Howe, James. The hospital book / by James Howe ; photographs by Mal Warshaw.   p.   cm.   Originally published: 1981. Summary: A guide to a stay in the hospital discussing what happens there, the people one meets, what will hurt, and how one gets better and goes home.   ISBN 0-688-12731-2.   1. Hospitals—Juvenile literature.   2. Children—Hospital care—Juvenile literature.   [1. Hospitals. 2. Medical care.]   I. Warshaw, Mal, ill.   II. Title.   RA963.5.H68   1994
362.1'1—dc20 93-15701   CIP   AC

For Betsy
J.H.

For my wife, Betty Weir,
who as a nine-year-old was president of the shut-in society;
and to our grandchildren Abigail, Matthew, Nicole, and Michael
M.W.

Contents

~~~~~~~~~~~~~

Acknowledgments

The Hospital Book would not have been possible without the cooperation and assistance of several New York City hospitals: their administrators, doctors, nurses, social workers, child-life specialists, volunteers, technicians, and other staff members and, most importantly, their patients and families. Their thoughts and experiences, which they shared generously, have helped shape this book.

Our thanks to Downstate Medical Center and New York University Medical Center. Much of our work in-depth was done with these two institutions, which opened their doors wide. Many people helped us along the way. At Downstate: the thoracic surgery team and operating room staff, the doctors, nurses and staff of the pediatric medical floor, Rita McNamara and Wilma Friday. At N.Y.U.: Dr. David Scotch, the doctors, nurses and staff of the pediatric floor, Joan Gildea, Lynn Odell, Katherine Wheeler and Linda Weissman.

St. Vincent's Hospital and Medical Center, where it began: Kathleen McQuade, Dr. Peter R. Scaglione, Ina Gellers, Rita Conyers, Alice Egland, Sister Marian Catherine, Geraldine Natwin and Mary Ann Going.

The Roosevelt Hospital: Dr. Louis Z. Cooper, Teri Lowinger and Peggy Ray.

Babies Hospital: Penny Bushman and Jane McConville.

Lenox Hill Hospital: Shirley Shufer and Harlan Conti.

Bellevue Hospital: Jim Walsh, Nancy Lewis, Vicki Ciampa and Pam McDonnell.

Norwalk Hospital: Dr. Robert Altbaum and Bruce Hutchison.

The Association for the Care of Children's Health; Children in Hospitals, Inc.; Susan Resnick; Dr. Ira Jaffrey; Mrs. Sandy Read Jaffrey; Children's Hospital of Washington, D.C., with a special thanks there to Doris Dellen and Lee Ann Slayton; the children and ex-children in our lives who reflected on their own experiences and responded to our work.

The children and families in the book who shared their hospital experiences with us—particularly Angela Drella and her mother, Marie Drella.

Stephanie Spinner for her guidance in the development of this book and Betsy Imershein for her invaluable help, insight and support.

A very special thank-you to Tina Quirk of Downstate Medical Center and the Association for the Care of Children's Health, whose limitless (or so it seemed to us) enthusiasm and support made possible much of what we saw and learned. We are deeply in her debt, and we hope that some of the spirit with which she infuses her work shines through in this book.

THE HOSPITAL BOOK

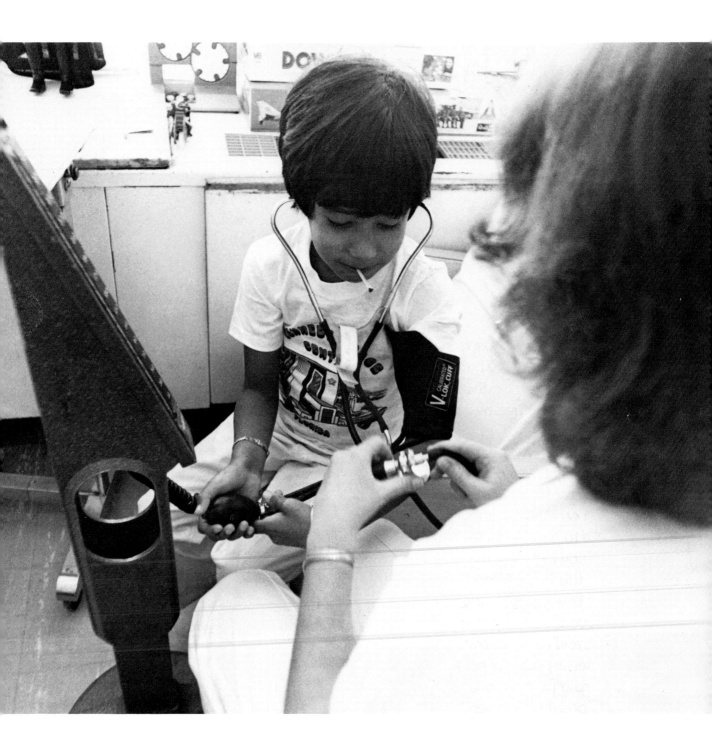

The Hospital

People go to the hospital for all kinds of reasons. Sometimes they have to be tested to find out what's wrong with them. Sometimes they are too sick to stay at home, and they need the attention of professional helpers day and night. And sometimes they need special medical treatment that only a hospital can provide.

When people have to go to the hospital, for whatever reason, they are often frightened or upset. They may be very sick or in pain. On top of that, they must face a new experience, leave home, sleep in a strange place and be taken care of by people they don't know. Naturally they worry about what is going to happen to them.

Knowing what the hospital is like can make it easier to be there. That's what this book is for: to tell you what happens in the hospital, whom you'll meet there, what kinds of things you'll see, what will hurt and what won't and how you'll get better and go home. Of course, no two hospitals are exactly alike, and your experience in the hospital may differ in some ways from what you see and read about in this book. The important thing to remember is that the main purpose of all hospitals is the same: to help you get better as quickly as possible, and send you back home where you belong, healthy again.

What Is Going to Happen to Me?

～～～～～～～

Your first stop in the hospital will be at the Admissions Office. Here you and your parents, or whoever takes you to the hospital, will be asked many questions about your health and your medical background. The information provided will help the hospital staff to take care of you. Also at this time your parents will fill out medical insurance forms and arrange to pay the costs of your stay.

Before you leave the Admissions Office a plastic wristband with your name on it will be fastened around your wrist. Wearing this will ensure that everyone in the hospital knows who you are, even when you're sleeping. When you put the wristband on you may feel like a "patient" for the first time, for you are now officially in the hospital's care.

Next you will be taken to the part of the hospital where you'll be staying. Though hospitals take care of people of all ages, children (everyone from newborn babies to people twenty-one years old) stay in the section called "pediatrics." Pediatrics is a special name for the medical care of children. Here you'll meet some of the nurses who will take care of you, and you'll be taken to your room.

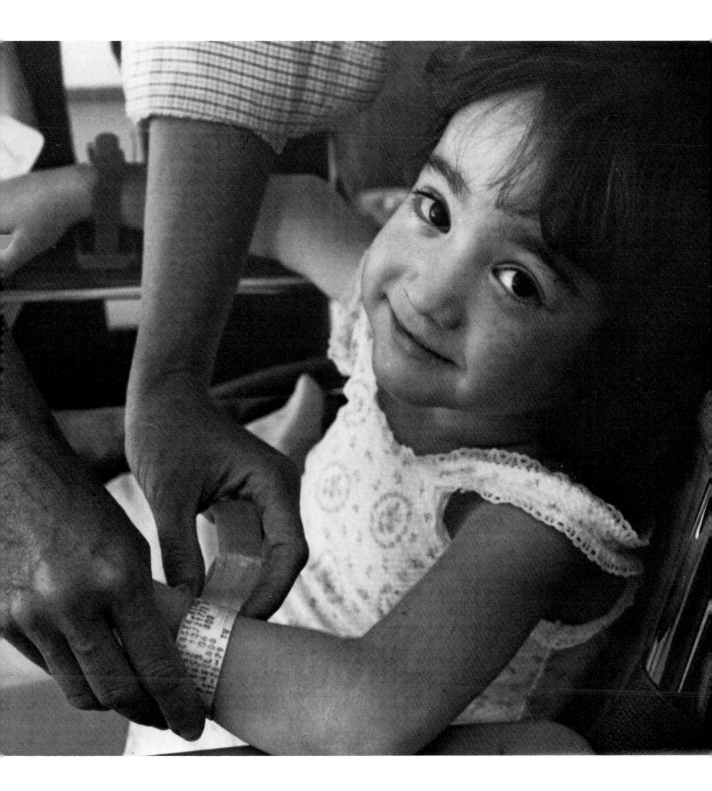

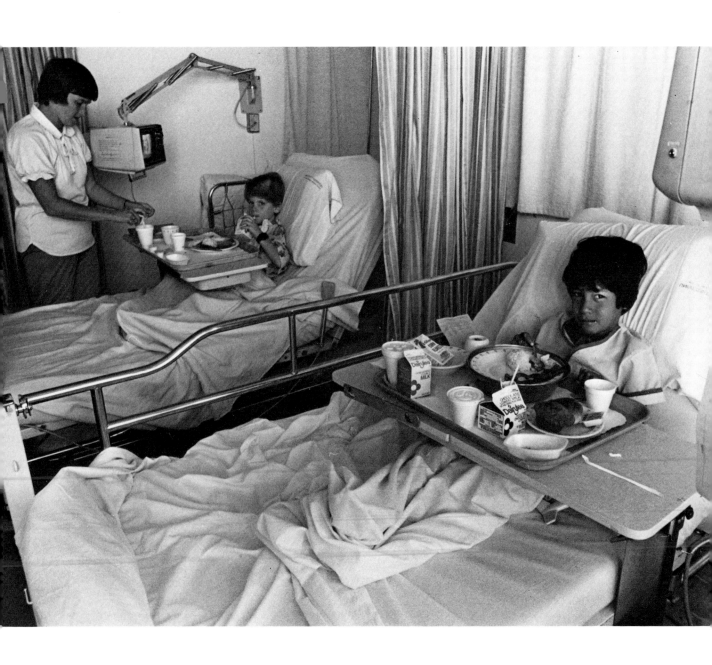

Most hospital bedrooms are for two or more patients, so it is likely that you'll be sharing a room with other children.

These boys are having dinner in bed, which is the way most people eat in the hospital. The tray they're eating on is called an over-the-bed tray. It's on wheels and can be rolled out of the way when it's not being used. And it can be used for more than just eating—it's good for writing or drawing on, or for resting a book on when you're reading.

The hospital bed is higher than your bed at home. Its height makes it easier for the doctors and nurses to take care of you without bending down.

The bed has guardrails at the sides to make sure that you don't fall out. Of course, you probably won't fall, but the rails are there for extra safety. Grown-ups' beds have them, too.

The hospital bed is also movable. A set of controls, either electric or hand-cranked, can make it go up or down. The section at the head can be raised, and so can the section at the foot of the bed.

The bed's mobility, like its height, makes it easier for people in the hospital to take care of you. It also helps to make you more comfortable. You can sit up in bed while you eat or read, like the patients in this picture.

The bedroom in this picture has television sets. Not all hospital bedrooms do.

In most hospitals each bedroom has its own private toilet. In some hospitals, however, there is one big bathroom with toilets for all the boys to use and another big bathroom with toilets for all the girls to use. In almost all hospitals there is a separate room for taking baths and showers.

Some hospitals have a schoolroom. Here, with the help of a teacher, you can keep up with your schoolwork or simply read about whatever interests you.

Many hospitals have a playroom filled with toys, games, crafts and play hospital equipment. The playroom is a good place for you to meet other children. You can also make things there to take home with you.

Some of the children in this picture are wearing their own nightclothes. Sometimes patients must wear hospital nightclothes, but most of the time they can wear their own.

This is a treatment room. It is something like a doctor's office or an examination room in a clinic. Patients are often examined and given simple treatments here. At other times these tests and treatments are done right in the patients' rooms.

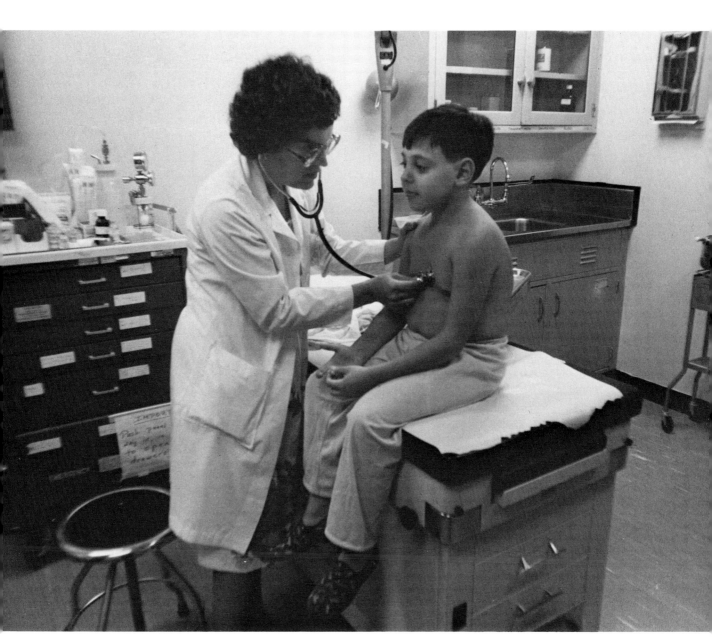

This area is the nurses' station. Nurses work here when they aren't working in patients' rooms. There are nurses at the nurses' station all day and all night. They will help you if you need something.

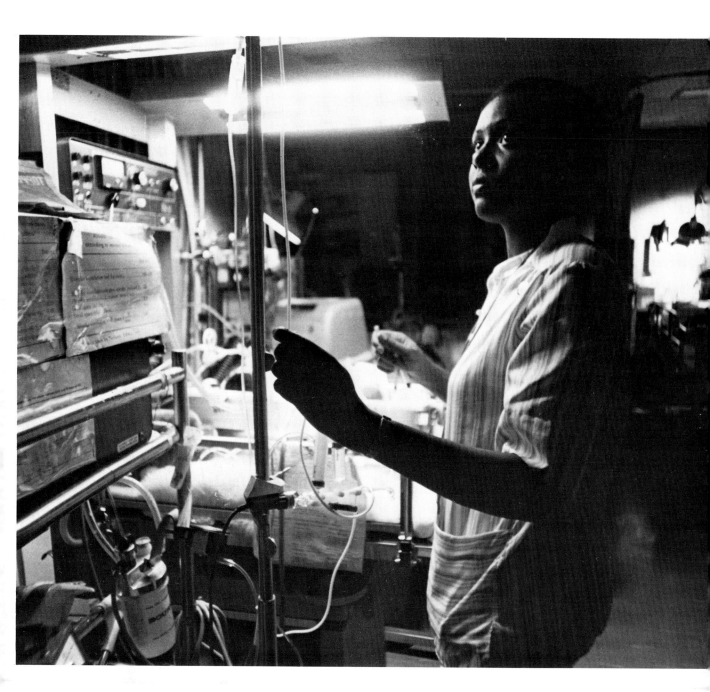

At night they will look into your room every once in a while just to make sure everything is all right. Nurses work in shifts of eight hours, so you won't have the same nurse at night as you do during the day.

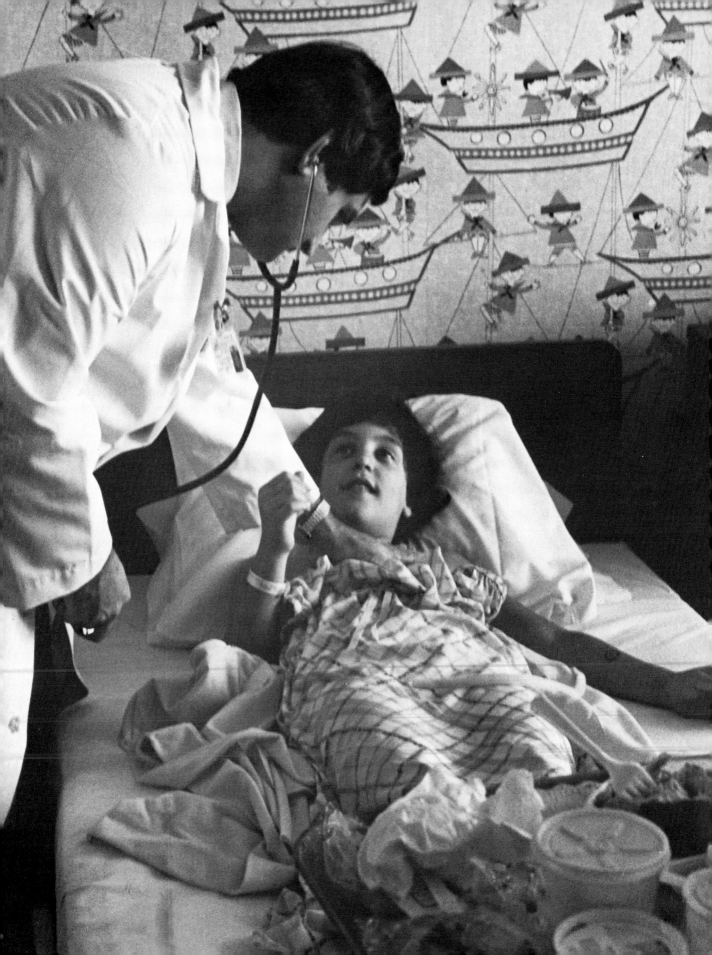

Soon after you've been taken to your room, a doctor or nurse will come to talk to you and ask you and your parents some questions. You'll be asked how old you are, what kinds of illnesses you've had before, whether this is the first time you've been in a hospital and many other questions about your health. This is called "taking your history," and it continues the process of gathering information that was begun in the Admissions Office.

The doctors and nurses will also get to know you better by performing some simple medical tests. These tests are given to all hospital patients, regardless of what is wrong with them, in order to check their general health. Most of the tests will take place in your room, although some may be done in the treatment room.

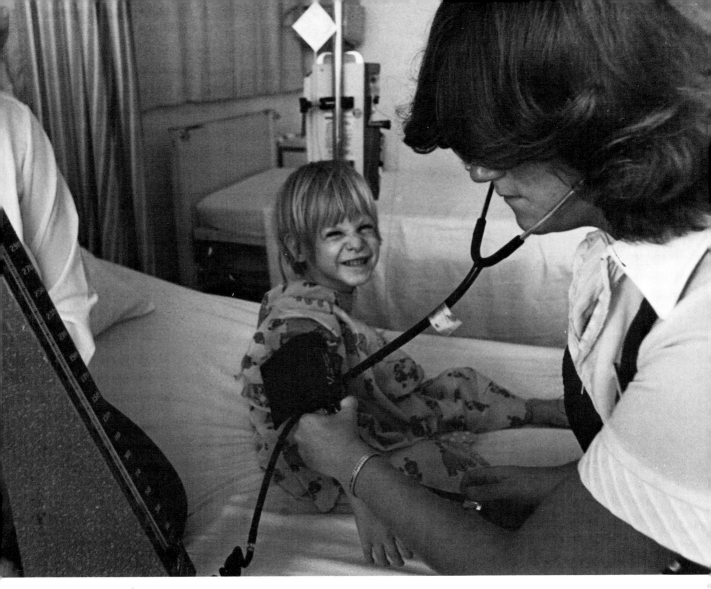

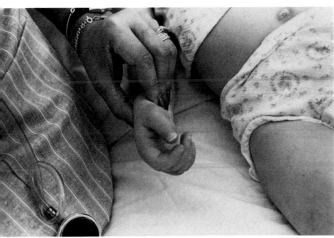

A nurse will take your temperature and your pulse. He or she will listen to your heart and lungs, take your blood pressure and check your height and weight. You will also be asked to give a sample of your urine and your blood.

For a urine sample the nurse will ask you to urinate into a plastic cup or bottle. The urine will then go to a laboratory, where it will be analyzed.

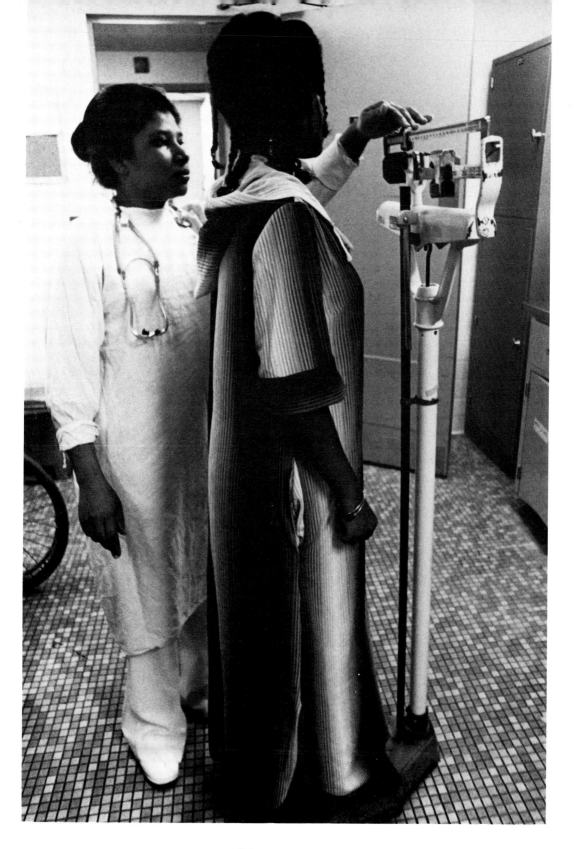

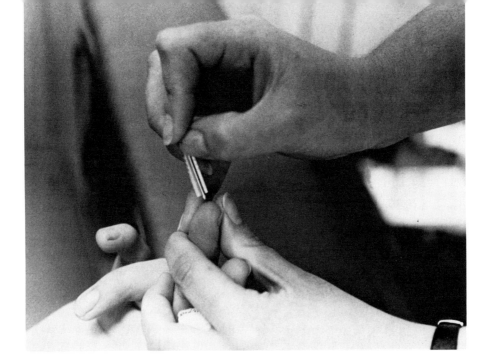

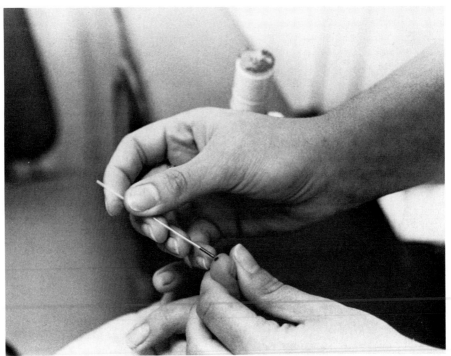

There are two ways of taking blood:

Sometimes one of your fingers is pricked. Then a thin glass tube is placed gently on the drop of blood on your finger, and the blood is drawn up through the tube.

At other times a needle is put into a vein in your hand or arm and blood is drawn out into a syringe, as it's being done in the picture.

Having a sample of your blood taken hurts, but only a little, and only for a few moments. You may have blood taken more than once, but no matter how much is taken, your body will always produce blood to take its place.

Like the urine sample, the blood will go to a laboratory where it will be analyzed. The urine and blood samples can tell doctors a lot about the general health of your body and whether or not there is disease or infection present.

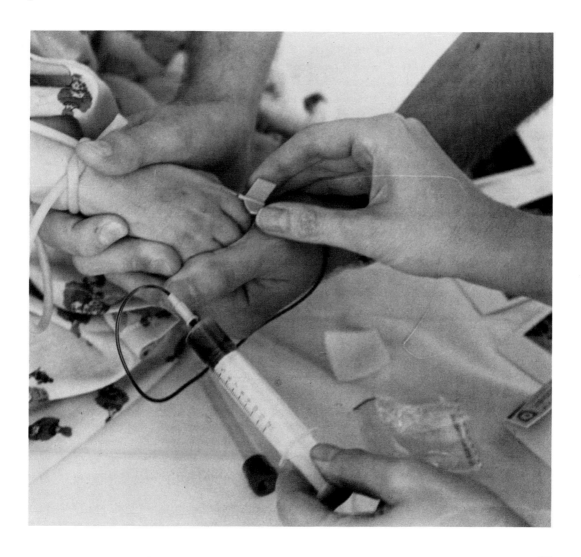

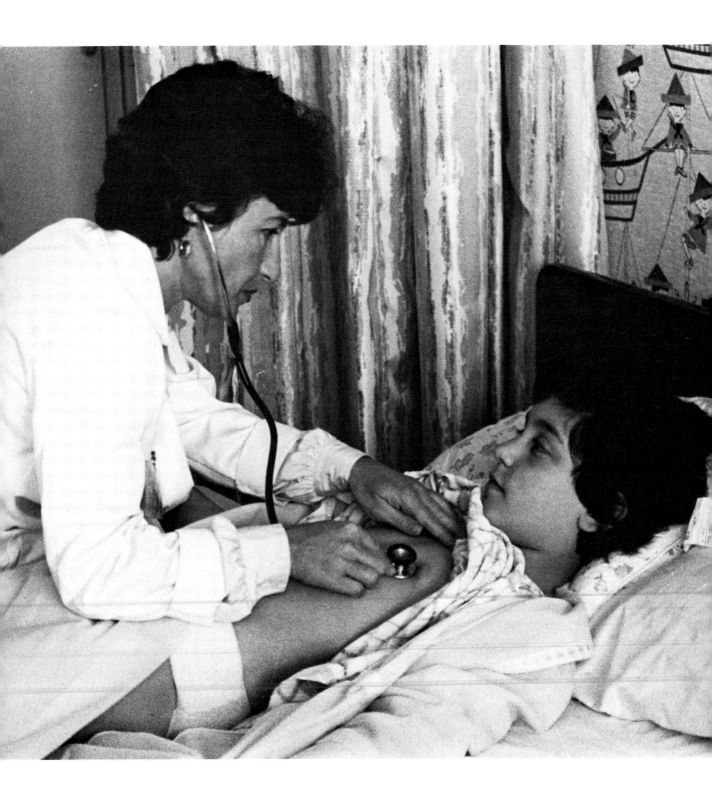

Who Is That Person?

~~~~~~~~~~

When you begin your hospital stay you may meet more people than you can keep track of. One recent study showed that new patients often met as many as fifty-two people during their first day in the hospital. That's a lot of people in such a short time! You may not meet as many, but you're sure to meet a good number. Some will come and go so fast that you won't even learn their names or what they do. Others, you will get to know.

One person you may know before you go to the hospital is your doctor. Or you may meet your doctor for the first time after you've been admitted. Either way, it is unlikely that you will see him or her more than once a day, and then only briefly. That's because doctors have many other patients in the hospital as well as patients to see in their offices.

There are other doctors who work in the hospital who will help your own doctor to look after you. These doctors are called "interns" and "residents."

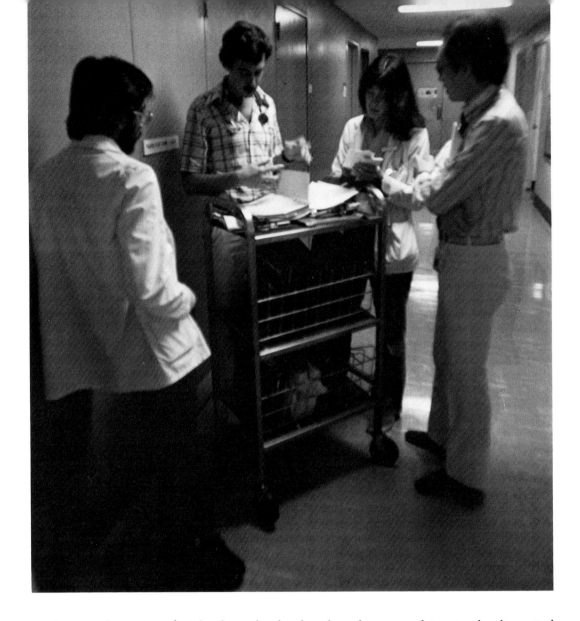

Interns have just finished medical school and are working in the hospital as part of their further training. Residents, who are more experienced than interns, supervise the interns' work with patients. Medical students in their last two years of medical school assist the residents and interns.

You will often see groups of doctors talking together in the hallways. They are "making rounds." The doctors will come into your room, stand around your bed and talk to you. They will also talk to each other about you. This is an important part of the young doctors' training. Doctors work together this way to learn from one another, and to help provide the best possible care for all their patients.

Nurses make rounds, too. These nursing students are going from room to room meeting with patients. They are discussing the patients with the nurse who is their teacher.

The nurse will spend more time with you than anyone else who works in the hospital. He or she makes sure that everything that is supposed to be done to help you get better is done.

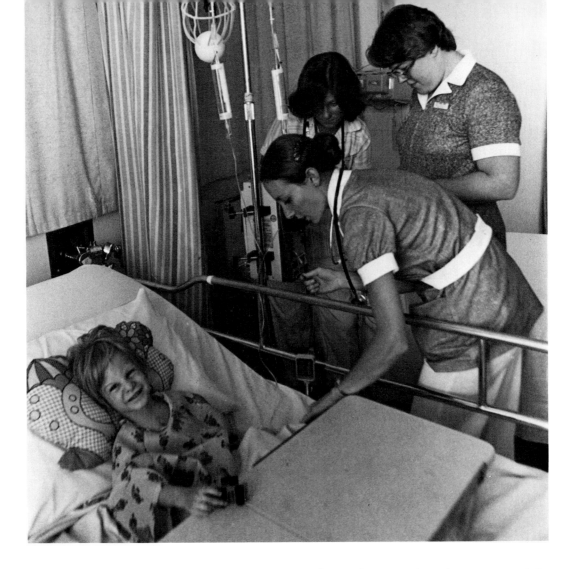

Nurses have a different kind of training from doctors, but they can and do make health-care decisions. They perform medical tasks such as giving injections and taking blood, and they can also answer questions about your illness and your treatment.

The nurse helps the doctor by gathering medical information and writing it down for the doctor to look at. The nurse also helps patients do things they may not be able to do by themselves, such as eating, washing and going to the bathroom.

Either the nurse or the nurse's aide will make your bed every day. The nurse's aide helps the nurse in many of his or her responsibilities. Aides cannot do anything medical, however, since they do not have any medical training.

This person is a laboratory technician. Laboratory technicians are trained to run some of the complicated machinery in the hospital. Here a lab technician is checking a monitor, a machine that keeps track electronically of a patient's heartbeat, breathing, blood pressure and temperature.

The laboratory technician is also trained to perform scientific procedures, such as blood tests. After the blood is taken from the patient, it goes to a laboratory in the hospital and it is the lab technician who looks at the blood cells under a microscope.

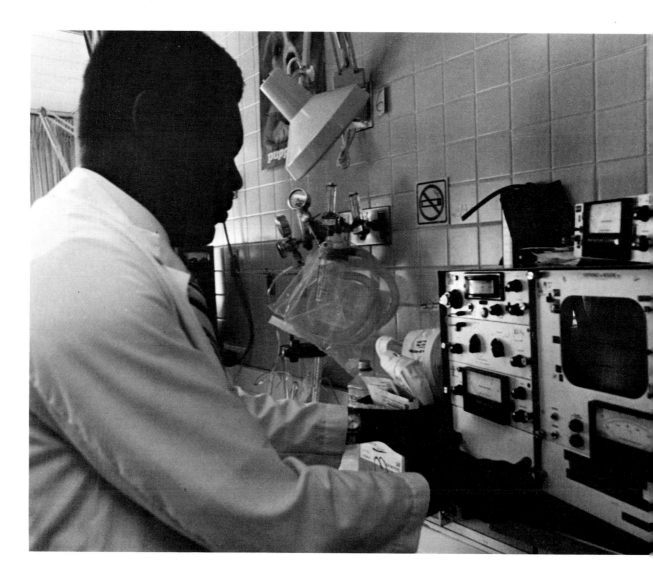

Hospitals often have people called "child-life specialists" who are in charge of the playrooms. Some hospitals have schoolteachers. These people may be helped by volunteers. Volunteers are not paid; they work in the hospital simply because they want to. Volunteers work with patients in many ways. They bring them water and juice, they play with them and read to them, and sometimes they just keep them company.

The dietician plans the meals of all the patients in the hospital. Sometimes people have to eat special foods because of the kind of illness they have. The dietician makes sure that they get the foods they need.

Many patients complain about hospital food. They say it doesn't taste very good. Sometimes, it doesn't. At other times it just doesn't taste like the food we're used to eating. Whether you like its taste or not, you can be sure it's good for you.

A custodian keeps the hospital very clean to help eliminate germs that can cause infection.

There are people we should talk about here even though they don't work in the hospital. These people are your parents.

Your parents are used to taking care of you, and it's not easy for them when you have to go to the hospital. Just as you'd rather be home, they would prefer to have you there. But while you're in the hospital they can visit, and perhaps even help with your care. Many hospitals allow mothers and fathers to look after their children in some of the ways they do at home, such as washing, dressing, or feeding them. There are even some hospitals that let mothers and fathers stay with their children overnight. This is not true of all hospitals, and whether your parents can do it depends both on their schedules and on the hospital rules. You can discuss this with your parents, and they can find out if the hospital allows overnight stays.

Whatever their rules about staying overnight, all hospitals have visiting hours, certain times of the day and early evening when patients can have a few visitors. Your parents will probably spend time with you then. Sometimes, though, they may be too busy caring for other members of your family or working to visit with you as often as you or they would like. At such times, remember that there is always someone on the hospital staff to look after you. In fact, the hospital is filled with people who are working to help you get better and feel as good as possible during your hospital stay.

What Is That Thing?

~~~~~~~~~~~~

In the hospital you will see a lot of things you may not recognize. All of them have something to do with helping you to get better.

A washbasin like the one on the right is used by the nurse or nurse's aide to help you wash when you can't get out of bed.

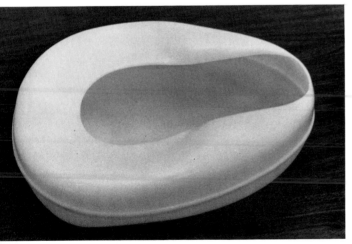

A bedpan is used for going to the bathroom right in bed. If you need to use one, the nurse will draw a curtain around the bed to give you as much privacy as possible. He or she will help you sit or lie on the bedpan, if you need help. This isn't the most comfortable way to go to the bathroom, but sometimes it is the only way.

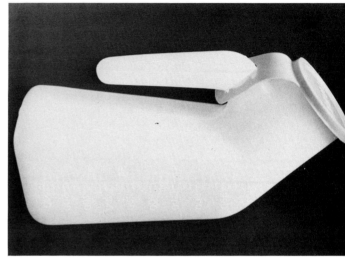

Boys use a urinal, like this, for urinating. But they use the bedpan, just as girls do, for bowel movements.

Another object you will see is an "emesis" pan. Emesis means throwing up. A pan like this is kept near each bed, should it be needed.

Though you'll probably see all of these things, you may not have to use any of them. You may not throw up while you're in the hospital, so you won't need the emesis pan. And you may be able to get out of bed during your entire stay, so you won't have to use the bedpan or the washbasin.

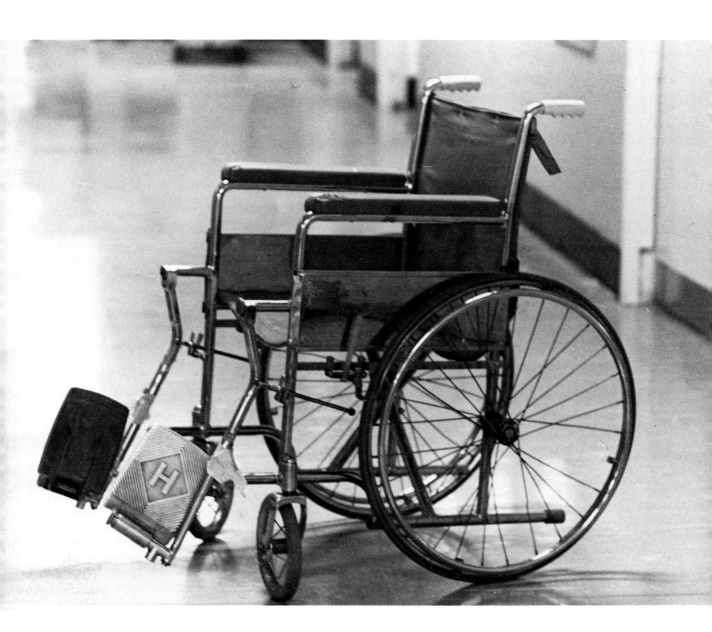

Not everyone who comes into the hospital has to use a wheelchair either. When a patient mustn't walk, but can sit up, he or she rides in a wheelchair. Usually, the patient can make the chair move, either by pushing the wheels or by pressing a control button that triggers the chair's movements electronically. But when the patient needs help, another person pushes the chair from behind.

40

A stretcher-bed is a bed on wheels. It is used to take patients to the operating room for surgery or to move patients around the hospital when they cannot sit up.

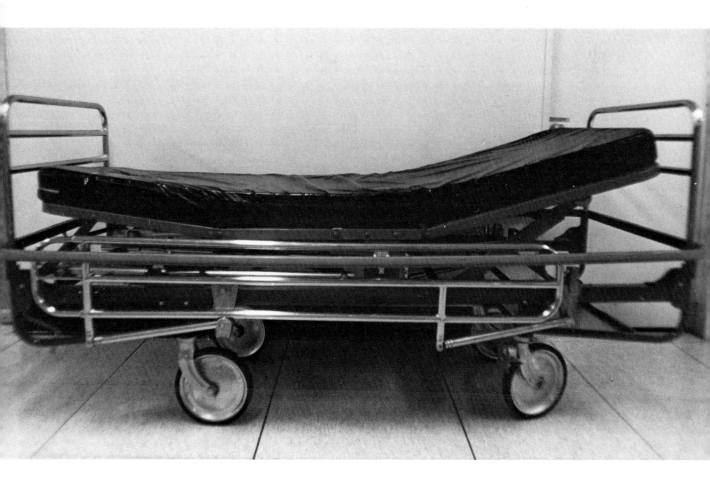

Some equipment in the hospital is for doctors and nurses to use when they try to find out what's wrong with a patient.

The stethoscope is used to listen to sounds inside your body, such as your breathing and your heartbeat. It makes these sounds louder. By placing the stethoscope on your chest, the doctor or nurse can hear how the air is moving in and out of your lungs. They can also hear if your heart is beating in a regular pattern.

The round part of the stethoscope may feel cold, because your skin has been under clothing and the stethoscope has been in the colder air. Usually the doctor or nurse will warm it up first, but sometimes they forget. You might ask to listen to your own or someone else's heartbeat with the stethoscope. Most doctors and nurses will be glad to let you.

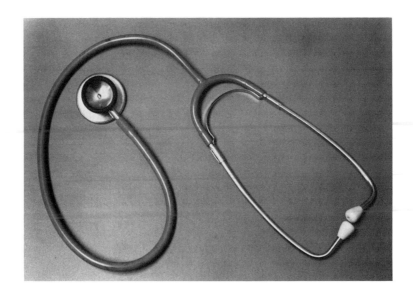

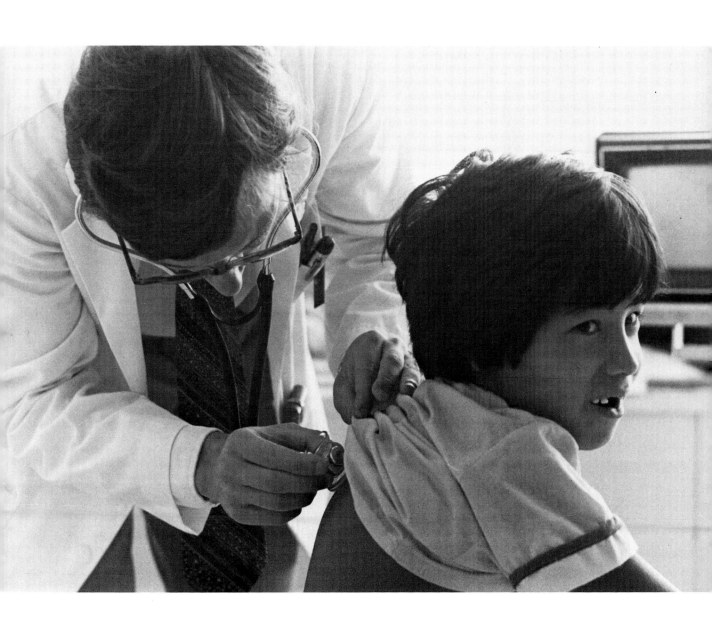

The otoscope is an instrument with a tiny flashlight inside it. It is used for examining the insides of your ears. The doctor or nurse puts one end of the otoscope into your ear and looks through the other end. This doesn't hurt, but it might tickle a little.

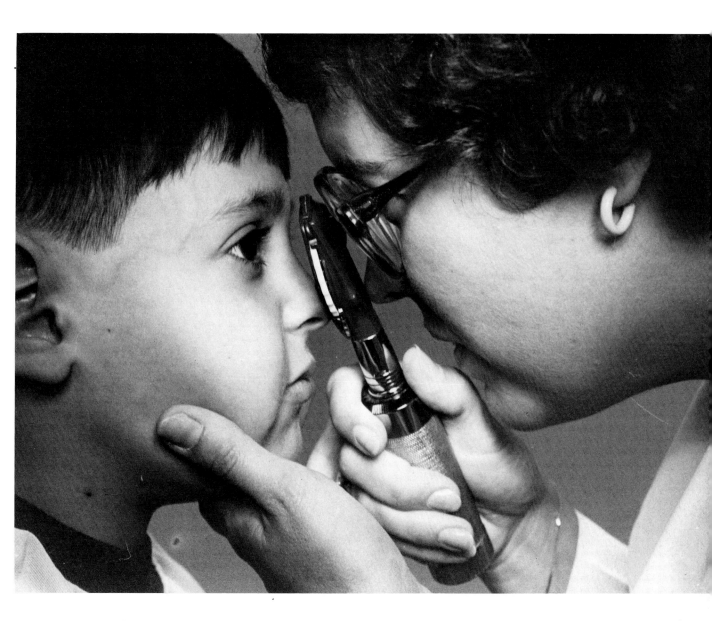

The ophthalmoscope is similar to the otoscope, but it is used for looking inside your eyes rather than inside your ears. Holding the ophthalmoscope up to your eye, the doctor or nurse can see right inside your eyeball to a large artery (a kind of blood vessel). Looking at this artery tells the doctor a great deal about the general health of your body.

The tongue depressor is a flat piece of wood that is used to keep your tongue down while the doctor or nurse examines your throat. The wood is dry and rough. When the doctor or nurse presses it against your tongue, you may feel like gagging. That's a normal reaction to the pressure.

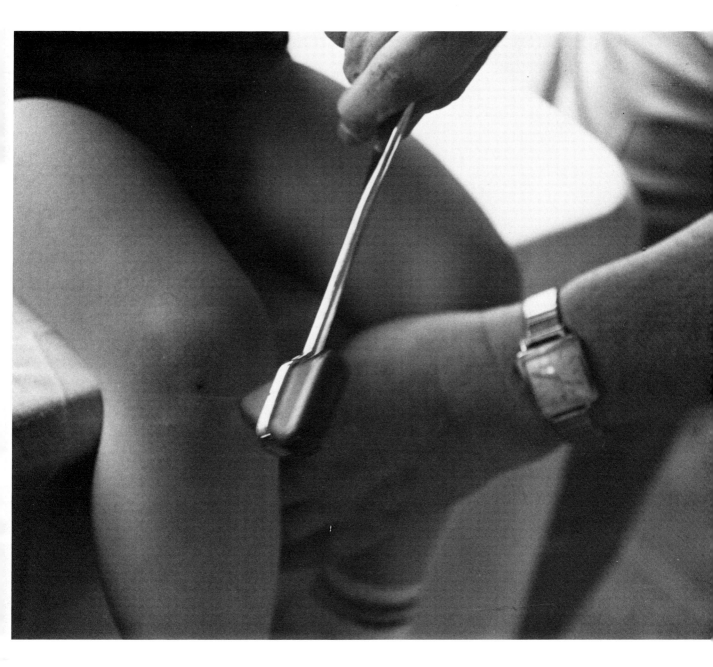

The doctor taps your knee or your elbow with a reflex hammer to see if your leg or arm will jump. This jumping is a normal way for your muscles to respond. Failure to jump may mean that there is a problem with the nerves that send messages to the muscles.

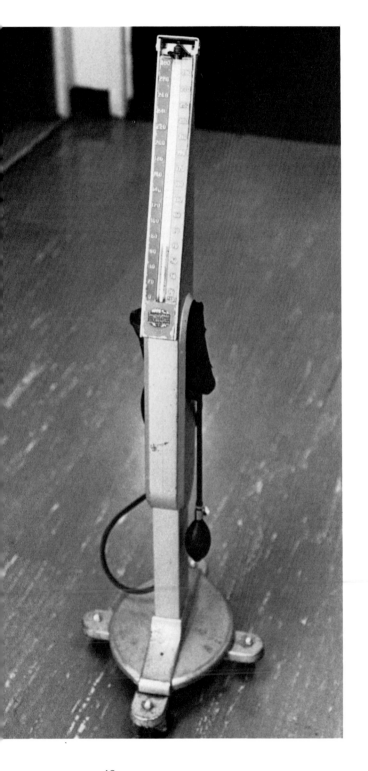

This is called a "sphygmoma-nometer." It is used to take your blood pressure. The nurse or doctor wraps a piece of cloth called a "cuff" around your upper arm. He or she then pumps air into the cuff so that it squeezes your arm tightly. This doesn't hurt, but you will feel pressure.

When the cuff is tight, the blood will stop flowing through the arteries at that place in your arm. Slowly, the nurse or doctor will let the air out of the cuff. When your blood starts flowing again, the nurse or doctor can listen to it by placing a stethoscope on the inside of your elbow. By listening to the sound of blood pumping through your arteries, they can find out how well your heart is sending blood through your body. Your blood pressure is taken quite often in the hospital—usually several times a day.

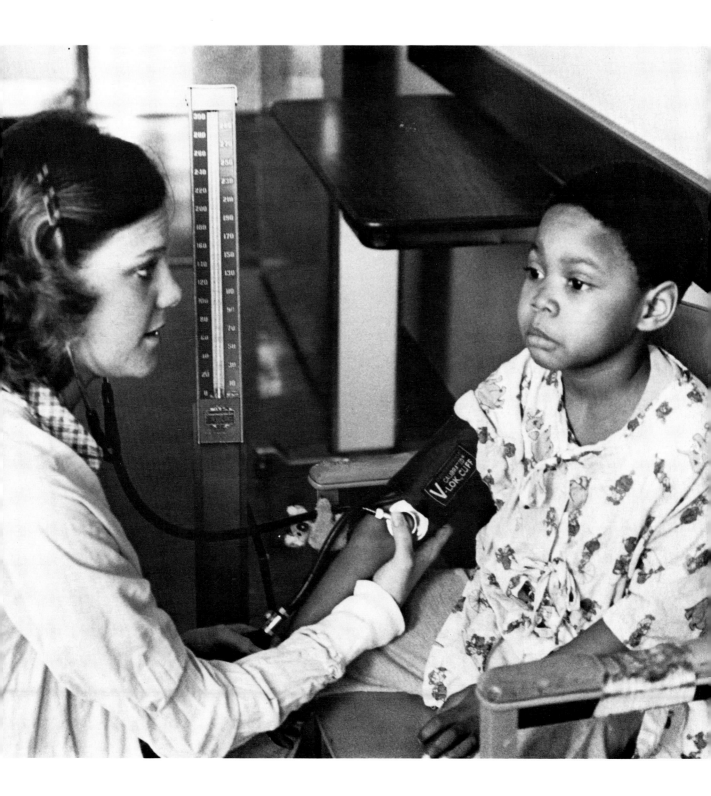

In the hospital your temperature is taken regularly, too. The thermometer measures your body's temperature. Normally, the temperature of the human body is 98.6° Fahrenheit or 37° centigrade. A higher temperature is often a sign of disease or infection.

Sometimes the thermometer is placed in the mouth under the tongue. At other times a different kind of thermometer, called a "rectal" thermometer, is used. This thermometer is put gently into the rectum, the opening where you have a bowel movement. An ointment is put on the thermometer first to help it go in easily. Though the rectal thermometer may feel a little uncomfortable, it will not hurt you.

Like everything in the hospital, both kinds of thermometers are cleaned very carefully after each use. Some hospitals use disposable thermometers that can be thrown away after one use.

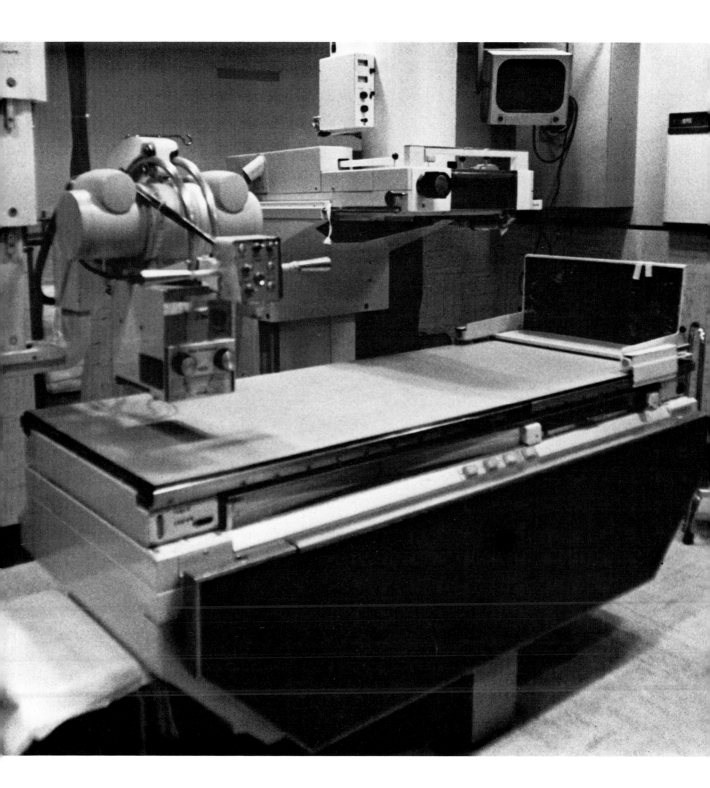

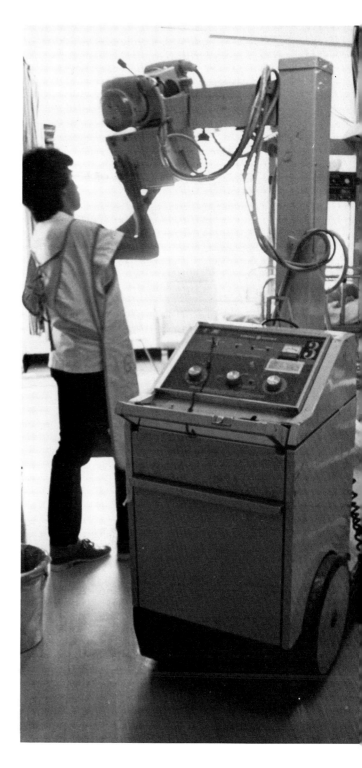

The X-ray machine is a special kind of camera that takes pictures of the inside of your body. To have an X ray taken, you must hold very still, so the picture will be clear. Being photographed by an X-ray machine doesn't take very long—and like getting your picture taken with an ordinary camera, it doesn't hurt. Most X-ray machines are in one place in the hospital: the X-ray or radiation department. The machines are operated by X-ray technicians.

The portable X-ray machine can be taken from room to room for use with those patients who cannot get out of bed.

There are many reasons for taking X-ray pictures. One of the most common is to find out if a bone is broken. If you've fallen out of a tree and your arm hurts, for example, the doctor will take an X ray to see if there is a break in the bone, and where it is located. Another reason for taking an X ray is to look at an area inside the body. A chest X ray, which is done on most hospital patients, shows the size, shape and position of the heart, as well as the general health of the lungs.

In an X ray the white parts you see are the very solid parts of your body, such as the bones and the heart. Organs and tissue such as your stomach, kidneys and lungs show up less clearly in X rays because they are less solid.

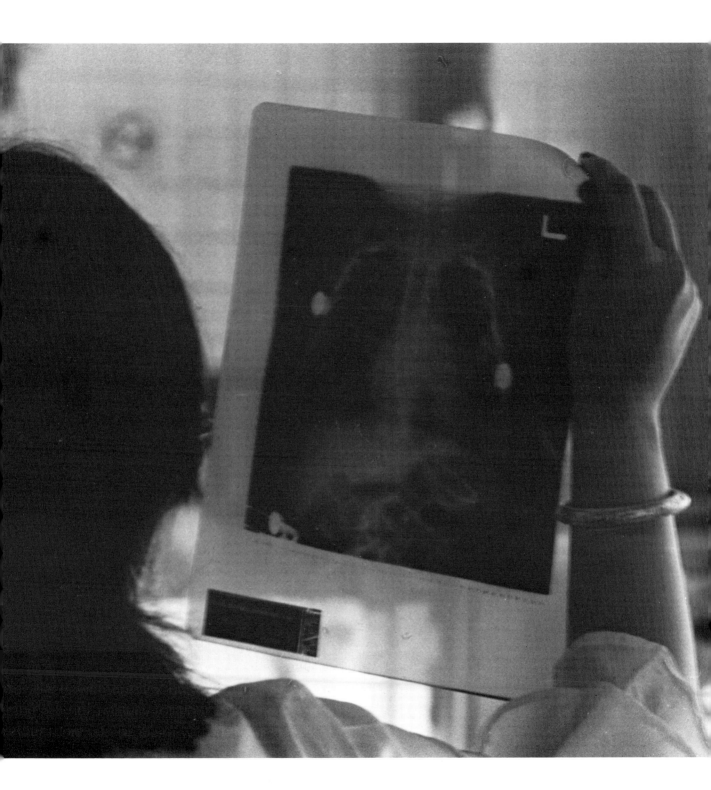

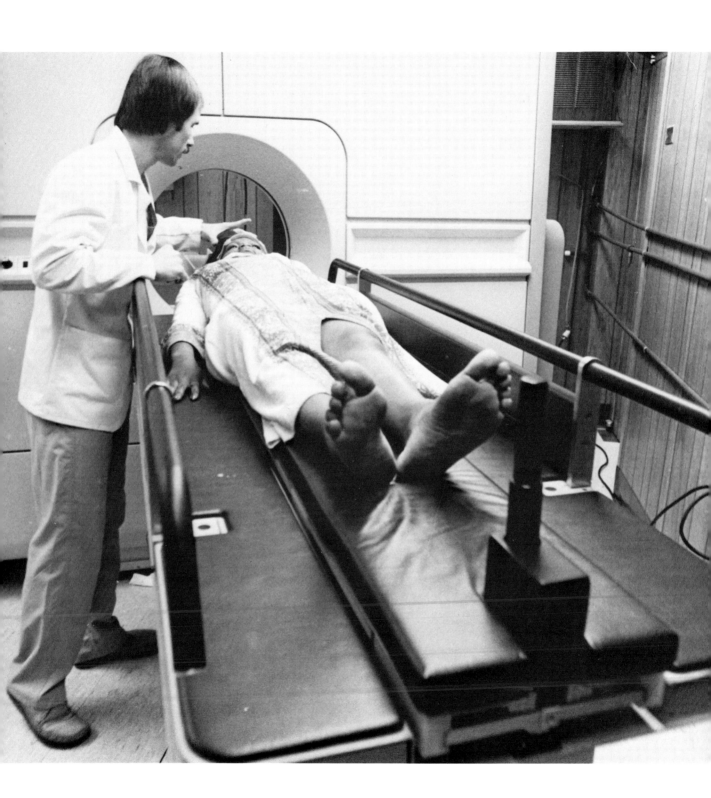

A special kind of X-ray machine called the "CAT scanner" (CAT is an abbreviation for computerized axial tomography) takes clearer, more detailed pictures of the body than an ordinary X-ray machine. The CAT scanner is used only when the doctor needs an extremely precise picture of part of a patient's body.

If you were having a CAT scan taken, you would lie down on the table, with your head on the raised headrest. Then your head or another part of your body—whichever area was being photographed—would be placed through the circle you see in this picture. The CAT scanner makes different noises while it takes its pictures, and the table moves up and down slightly to allow the scanner to photograph at different angles. Nothing hurts you while this is going on, but a CAT scan takes longer than normal X rays, so lying still for a long time can become uncomfortable.

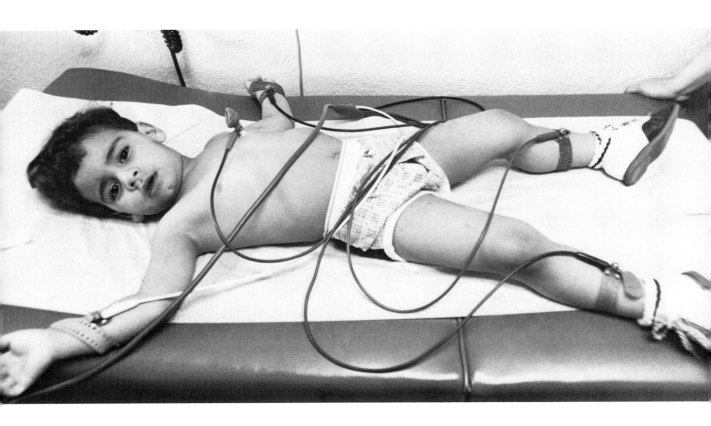

The electrocardiogram machine (usually called an ECG or EKG machine) tests the health of your heart. Small pieces of rubber, which look like suction cups, are placed on your body in different spots. These pieces of rubber, called "leads," are held on tightly by a kind of gelatin that is dabbed on your skin first. This may feel cold and clammy but it does not hurt. The leads are attached by wires to the machine, which records your heart's rhythm on a chart, as well as the force of each heartbeat.

58

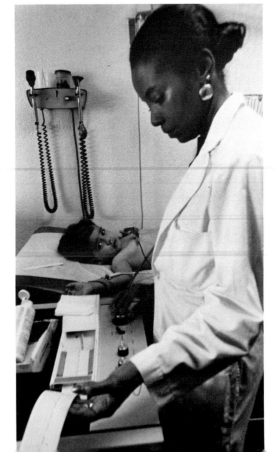

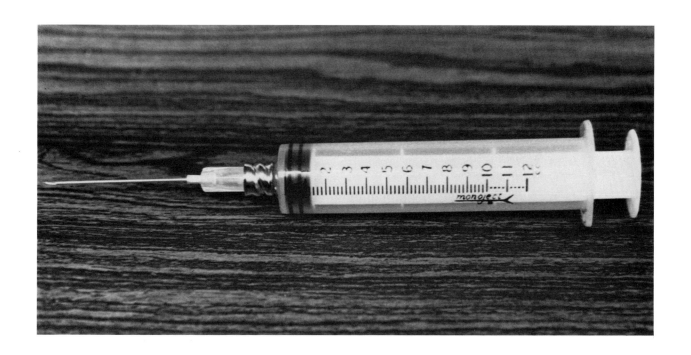

The needle is used for a variety of reasons. It is sometimes used to take blood, and other times to give medicine.

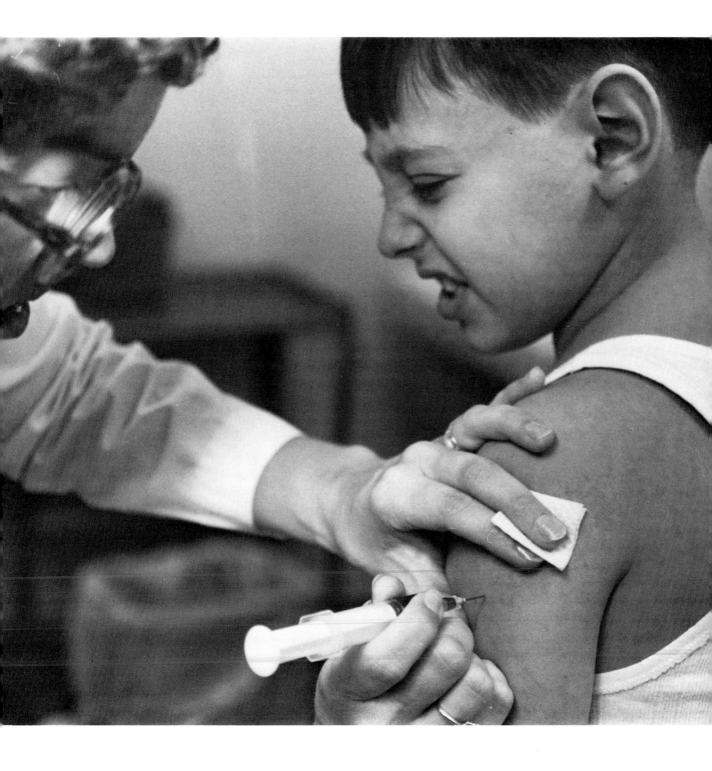

How Will I
Get Better?

~~~~~~~~~

In the hospital there are many ways of helping patients to get better. In fact, providing a wide variety of treatments to sick people is one of the most important things a hospital does.

Medicine is one kind of treatment. You may be given medicine in pill or liquid form. Or you may be given medicine with a needle.

This needle is being used to give an injection (or "shot") of medicine. When the doctor or nurse puts the needle through the patient's skin and pushes the plunger, the medicine goes through the needle and directly into the patient's bloodstream. When it is given this way, medicine starts working immediately.

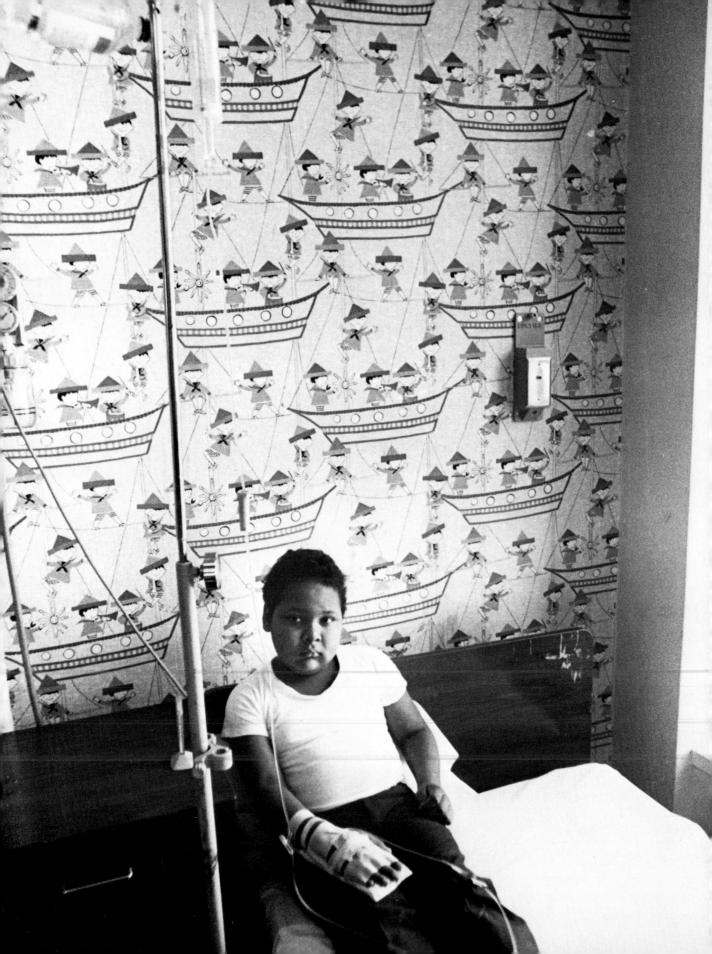

When small amounts of medicine must be given to a patient slowly over a period of hours or even days, an IV is used. IV is the short way of saying "intravenous," and it refers to the equipment that makes it possible for medicine to go within (*intra*) the vein (*venous*). IVs are not always used to give medicine, however. When illness prevents a patient from eating solid food or from drinking, an IV is used to provide liquid nourishment in the form of sugar and water. Intravenous feeding, like intravenous medication, may go on for many hours and even many days.

If your doctor decides you need an IV, here is what will happen:

A needle will be put into your vein. It will be taped carefully to your arm or leg to keep it from falling out. Your arm or leg may be taped to a board to make the IV even more secure.

The needle is attached to tubes that lead to plastic bags or bottles containing liquid. The containers hang on a pole that stands next to your bed. The liquid in the container drips, drop by drop, into the tube and from there through the needle into your vein.

If the dripping stops, or the needle comes out, nothing will happen to you. The doctor or nurse will simply start the IV up again or replace the needle.

It's not difficult to get used to an IV. The needle may hurt when it first goes in, but it will not continue to hurt. Once it's in, you can use your hands and move around easily, and if you're able to get out of bed, you can wheel your IV pole down the hall right along with you.

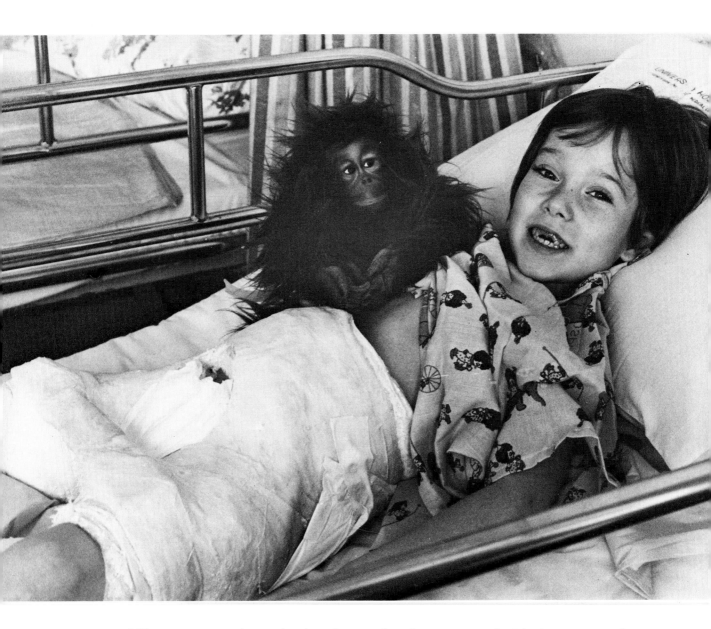

When a patient has a broken bone, the doctor may decide to use a cast. A cast is a bandage made of plaster. It holds broken bones in place so they can grow back together properly.

The boy in this picture is wearing a hip cast. He has to stay in bed for quite a long time because it is difficult to move in such a big cast. It helps him to have a friend for company—even a friend who is a gorilla.

When people have trouble breathing and their bodies don't get all the oxygen they need, they are given extra oxygen by machine. The machine in this picture is called an I.P.P.B. machine. I.P.P.B. stands for Intermittent Positive Pressure Breathing. It is often used to help patients breathe after they have had surgery in their chest area. The machine is used for about five minutes every four or five hours to help the patient's lungs push out.

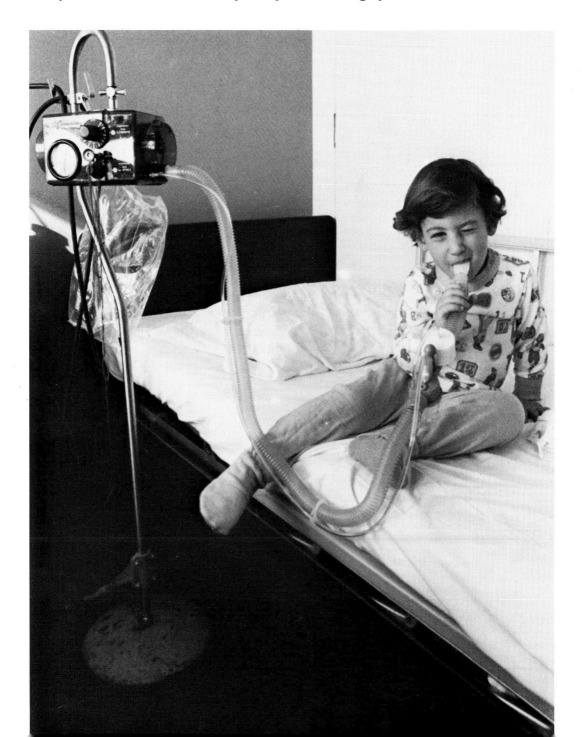

One kind of treatment that worries everyone is surgery. Having surgery is also called "having an operation." If you're not going to have surgery, nothing that is described here will happen to you. If you're unsure whether or not you are going to have surgery, ask your parents or your doctor, so that you'll know—and so that you can talk about it with them if you want to.

There are two reasons for surgery to be done. It may be necessary for the doctor to take a close look inside your body to get a better idea of what is wrong with you. Or if the doctor knows what is wrong, he or she may need to operate in order to make it better.

A few special things will be done to get you ready for surgery. First of all, you won't be allowed to eat anything on the day of the operation. This is because the anesthetic that is given during surgery can make you feel sick to your stomach. So it is better not to have any food in your stomach to begin with.

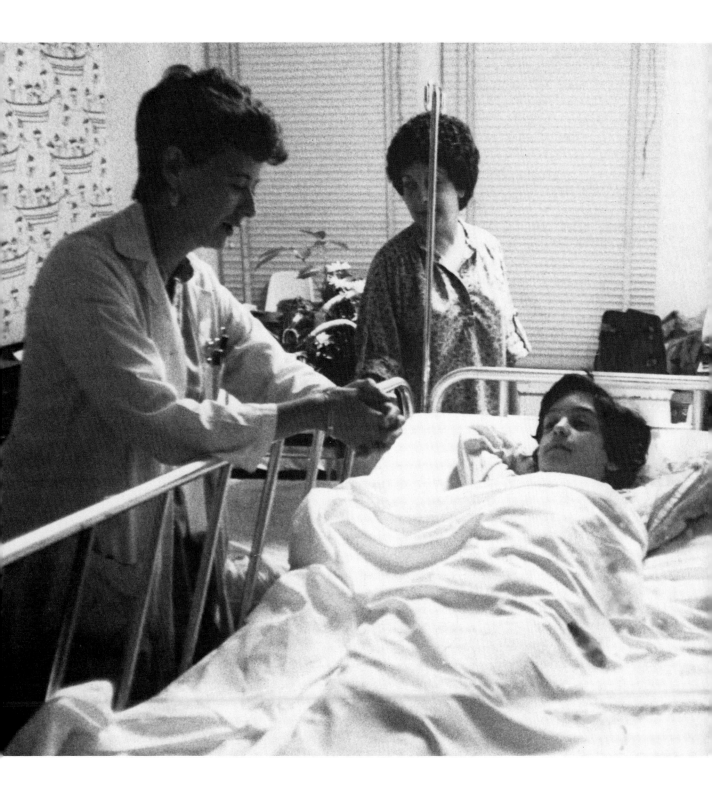

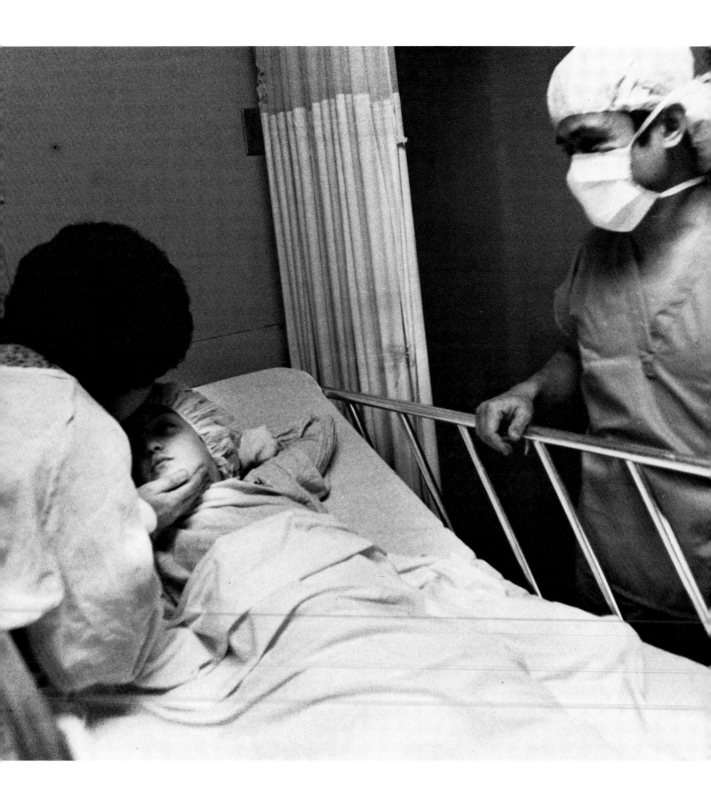

You will be washed or asked to wash yourself very thoroughly. You will take one or even two baths and will be asked to scrub with a special liquid soap. All of this washing is to help prevent any chance of infection during the operation.

You will wear special clothes to go into the operating room. These include a hospital gown and a cap that looks like a shower cap.

About an hour before you go to the operating room, you will be given medicine by injection to help you relax. This medicine will probably make your mouth feel quite dry. It may also make you feel slightly drowsy. After the injection someone from the operating room will come to your room and talk with you about what is going to happen.

Then another person from the operating room will come with a stretcher-bed to take you to the surgical floor. The operating room (sometimes called "O.R." for short) is usually on a different floor of the hospital, so riding to the O.R. may include a trip in the elevator. Your parents can come with you.

In many hospitals you won't go right into the O.R., but will stop first in a "holding room." Usually, your parents can come in with you. There will be other patients waiting for surgery in the holding room.

Almost all hospitals have more than one O.R.; while you're having your operation, other patients will be having operations nearby.

After a short wait you will be taken into the operating room. Your parents cannot go into the O.R. with you. They will wait in a room nearby or in your hospital room.

The operating room, with its tiled floors and walls and shiny metal machinery, is not a very friendly looking place. But its hard surfaces are easy to keep clean and free of germs and all its machinery helps the doctors and operating-room staff. What makes the O.R. a little warmer is the people who work there. These people are waiting and ready to take care of you just as soon as you arrive.

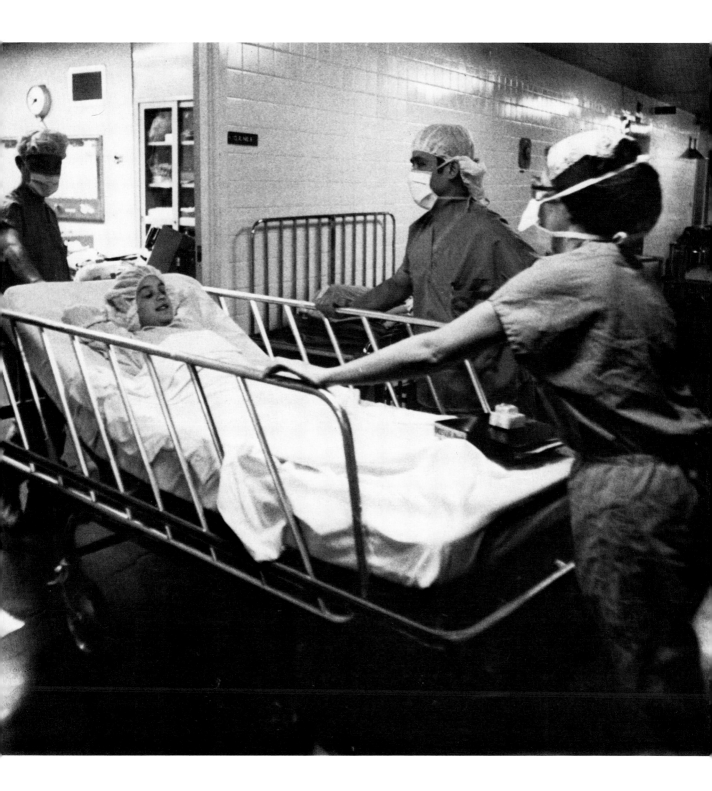

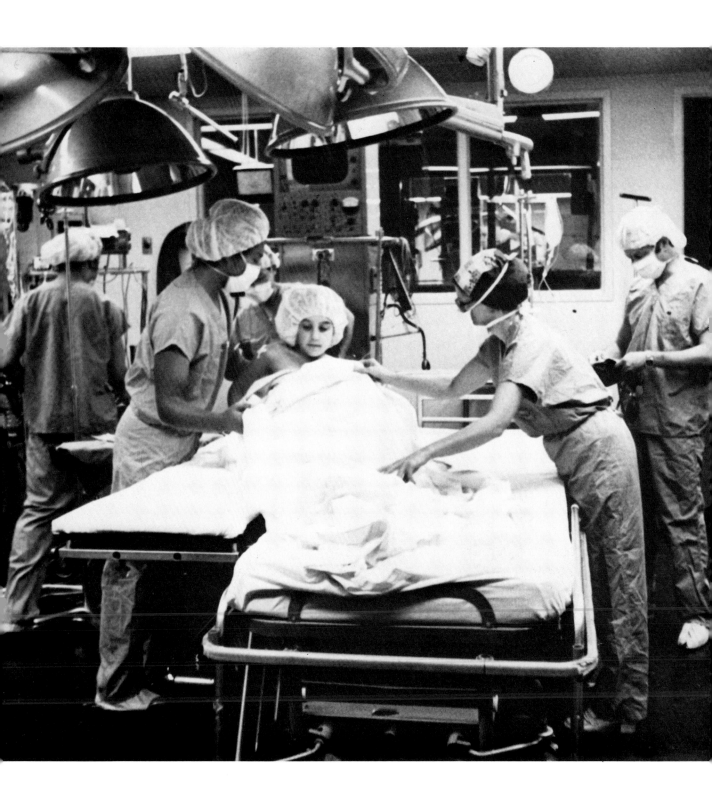

The doctors, nurses and technicians who work in the operating room wear blue or green shirts, pants, caps, shoe coverings and masks. Like everything else in the O.R., all these pieces of clothing are sterile, which means they are free of germs. Sterile clothing and equipment help to prevent infection of any kind.

Although people in the O.R. wear masks and their mouths are covered, they can still talk with you, and you can still see the care and concern in their eyes.

Once you get to the O.R. you will be helped off the stretcher-bed onto the operating table. You may be aware of the big lights hanging over the table. These are special lamps that help the doctors see very clearly. While the people around you prepare for the operation, they will talk to you.

One person who will talk to you right away is the anesthesiologist. He or she is a doctor and will sit right behind your head during the operation. The anesthesiologist will give you a medicine called an "anesthetic," so that you will not feel any pain during surgery.

One kind of anesthetic you may be familiar with is Novocain. If you've ever had a cavity filled at the dentist's office, you've probably had an injection of Novocain. You know that the Novocain made the area around your tooth numb, so that when the dentist drilled, you didn't feel anything. In a similar way the anesthetic given to you by the anesthesiologist will make your body numb, so that you won't feel anything during the operation.

There are two kinds of anesthetic given for surgery: local and general. You will be given one or the other.

A local anesthetic is injected into the area of the body where surgery will be done. The patient is awake during the operation, but feels no pain.

A general anesthetic numbs the patient's entire body, including the brain. This causes a kind of sleep called "unconsciousness," which lasts throughout the entire operation.

A general anesthetic is sometimes given with an IV so it goes directly into the bloodstream, and sometimes given in the form of gas, which is inhaled through a mask.

The patient in this picture is being given a general anesthetic.

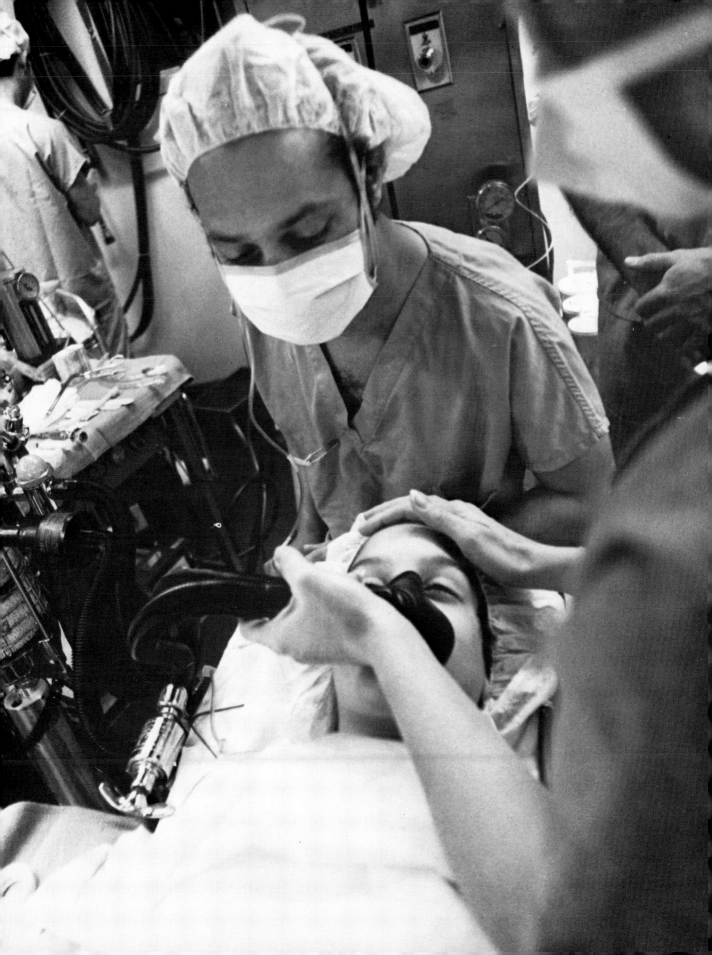

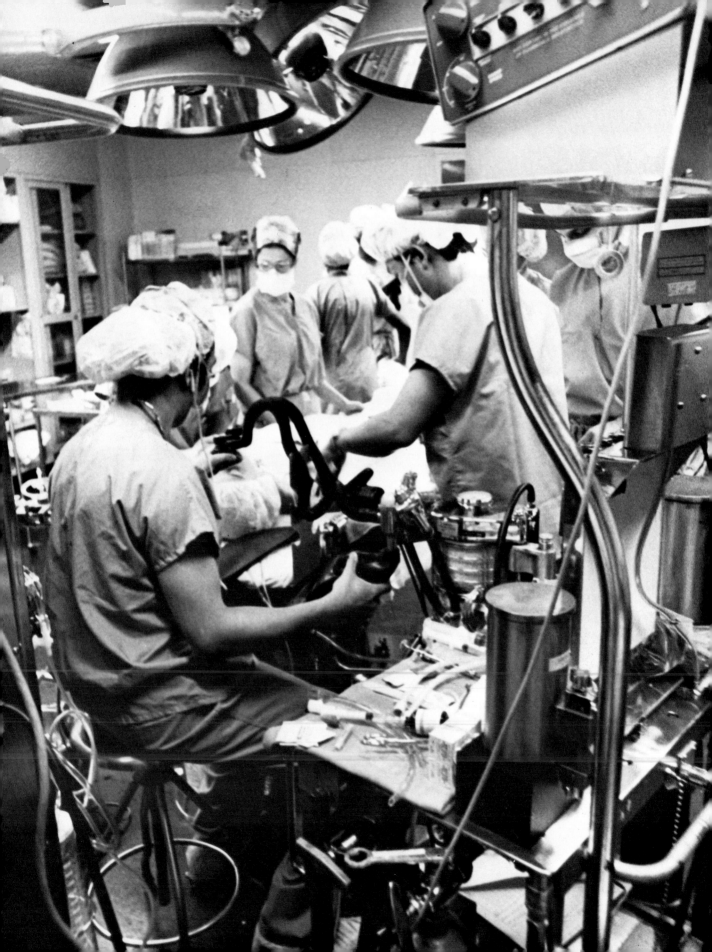

If you are given a general anesthetic, you will continue to receive it during the operation, and you won't wake up until after the operation is over. As soon as you are unconscious, the doctors, nurses and specially trained technicians will go to work.

To operate, the doctors must make an opening, or incision, in your body. The idea of being cut open is frightening to everyone. Some of the fear comes from thinking we'll feel pain when we're cut open. Some of it comes from thinking we might wake up and see something upsetting. In fact, you won't see or feel anything during your operation. It's also important to remember that only the part of your body that must be cut will be.

After the surgery has been done, the doctor will close the incision using special threads and needles. He or she will sew the layers of muscle and skin back together tightly and cleanly. You will have stitches where the doctor has sewn.

You will then be taken on a stretcher-bed to the "recovery room." If you have been given a general anesthetic, you will still be unconscious at this point.

In the recovery room you will be watched very carefully by the doctors and nurses to make sure you are all right. As soon as you wake up, you will be taken back to your room.

You may be taken to the Intensive Care Unit instead of the recovery room if your particular illness or surgery requires you to be watched for more than a few hours. In the I.C.U. (as the Intensive Care Unit is called for short) there are many doctors, nurses, technicians and machines to watch over just a few patients. When your doctor decides that you are ready, you will be returned to your own room.

You probably will not feel very well when you wake up after surgery. You may not know where you are at first. You may ache. Your stomach may be upset and you may feel like throwing up. These feelings will pass fairly quickly, but you will be tired for a while. And it will be some time before you're full of energy again.

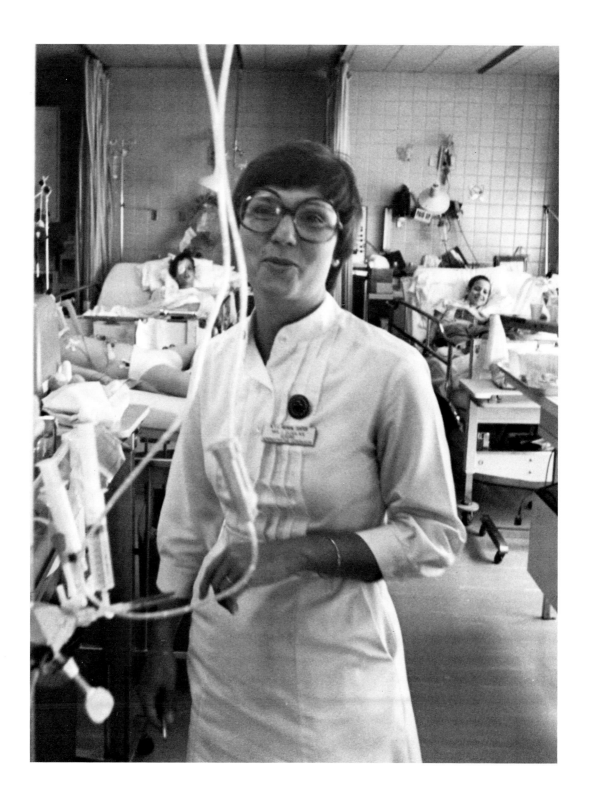

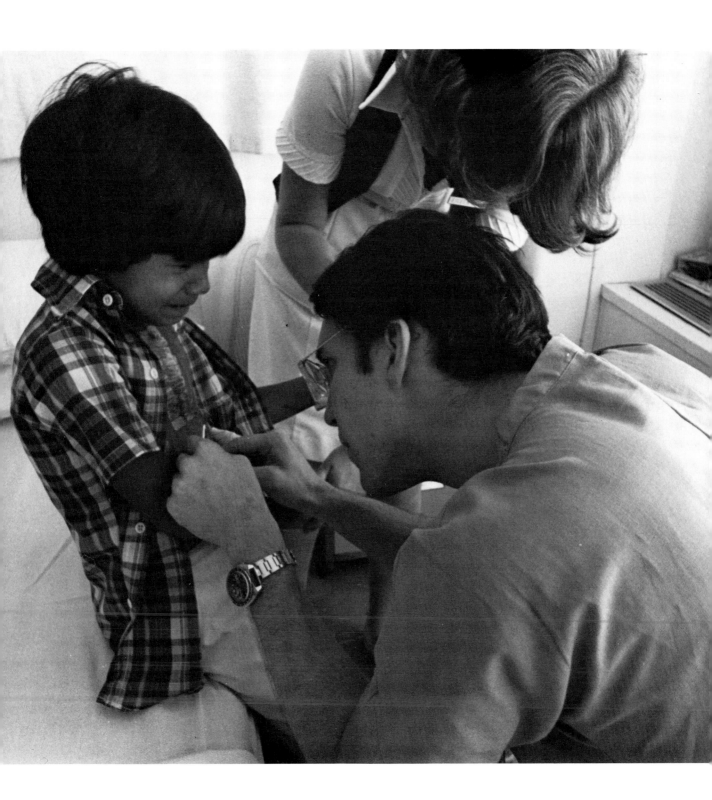

After a few days the stitches from where the doctor sewed you up will be removed. There will be a scar where the incision was made. When you first see the scar it may be red and swollen, but it will not stay that way for long. The redness and swelling will go down, and after a while the scar will be only a thin line.

The boy in this picture is having stitches removed from his chest. It hurts, but only a little and only for a short time.

How Will I Feel?

Being in the hospital can be a difficult and painful experience, both physically and emotionally. Physical pain is something no one likes. Unfortunately, it is almost always a part of being sick or injured. It is often a part of getting better, too.

Not everything that happens in the hospital will hurt you. In fact, most things won't. But some things do hurt, and knowing what they are can help you to deal with the pain.

Many people, including grown-ups, find the idea of being stuck with a needle especially frightening. This can become a problem, since needles are used so often in the hospital. The truth is that needles do hurt, and it is perfectly all right to express the pain you feel when you get an injection. You can say "Ouch!" or squeeze somebody's hand. Or you can cry if you feel like it. Because needles hurt, and no one expects you to pretend that they don't.

If you're having surgery, you will probably hurt for a while after the operation. Your body has to heal, and that won't happen without some pain.

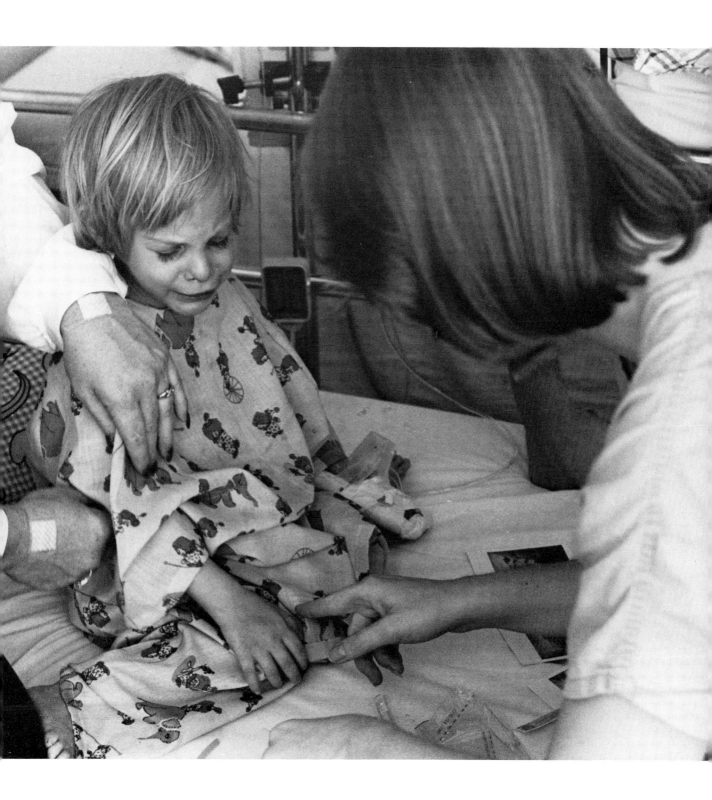

The doctors and nurses know this. They will give you medicine to stop the pain or ease it, the way aspirin helps to ease the pain of a headache.

In the hospital, medicine to lessen pain is not only given after surgery. It is given to ease other kinds of pain as well. But even with such medicine, your body may hurt for a time.

Different kinds of tests and treatments are done in the hospital, and some of these hurt. We've talked about a few of them in this book, but we can't discuss them all because there are so many different kinds. So if you are going to have a test or treatment that you've never had before, you can ask what it is, and then ask, "Will it hurt?" That way you can be ready for it to hurt if it's going to.

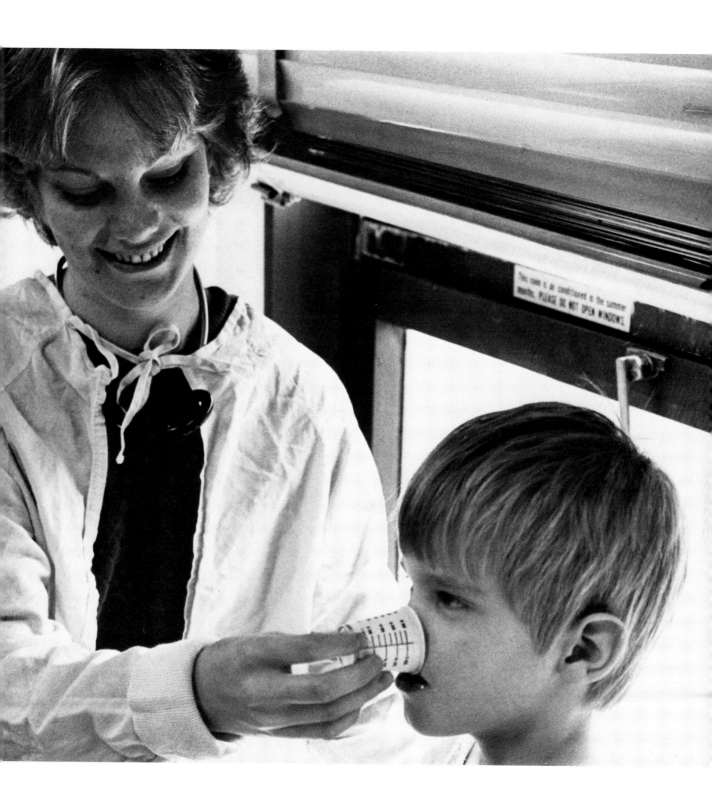

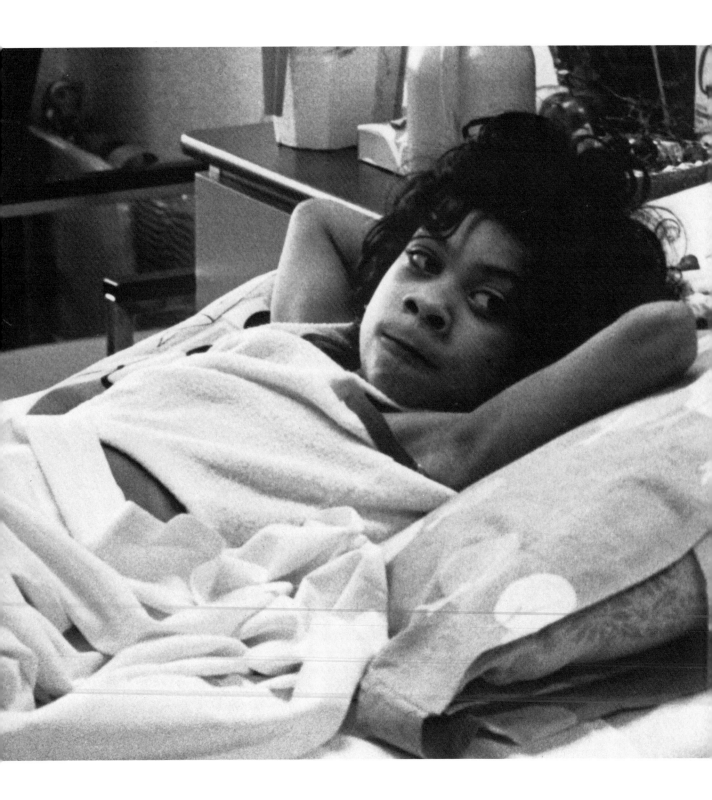

No matter how prepared you are, being hurt can make you angry. Anger is a difficult feeling to handle. You might feel that you shouldn't be angry, that it isn't nice or that you're not a good person if you get mad. But when you think about it, there are lots of real reasons to feel angry when you're in the hospital. And the people there understand that you can't always keep your anger inside.

Just being ill or injured can make you angry. Although it's normal for everyone to be sick from time to time, and although accidents can happen to anyone, it still may seem unfair when it happens to you. That's a normal reaction. The truth is, no one wants to be sick; it just happens, and there's nothing fair about it.

Another thing that might make you angry is having to do things the way other people want you to do them, instead of the way you're used to doing them. You may have to eat special foods or stay in bed for long stretches of time, or change your habits in some other way. No one likes changes in routine, but they are often a necessary part of getting better.

Still, in the hospital you may feel that you don't have a say in your own life anymore. People walk in and out of your room day and night, without even bothering to knock. Just when you want to watch television or eat your lunch, somebody comes in to stick a needle in your arm or put a thermometer under your tongue. And maybe the nurse who is usually so nice suddenly snaps at you. Or the doctor doesn't really listen when you ask a question. Perhaps the doctor or nurse tries to put the needle for an IV in your arm and can't find the vein right away. It hurts, although no one means it to, and you may feel angry about it.

Everybody tries to make being in the hospital as pleasant as possible, but people are people. Sometimes they're rushed or tired, sometimes they're not such nice people to begin with and sometimes they don't do things the way you would do them yourself. So you feel angry. What can you do about it?

The first thing to do is to tell someone. When you feel it, say, "I'm really angry now." Talk about it until you start to feel better. You'd be surprised— just talking can help a lot of angry feelings go away.

Crying can help, too. People are often afraid to cry because they are told that crying is for babies. Crying does not make you a baby, no matter what anyone says. There are times when people feel so bad that they can't express their feelings in words. At those times, crying helps.

But what if you feel even angrier? That you'd like to hit someone or something? Hospital playrooms usually have punching dolls, hammer toys, play hospital equipment, clay to pound, paper to draw angry faces on—all sorts of things to help you express your anger. These are safe ways to express it, so you don't hurt yourself or anyone else.

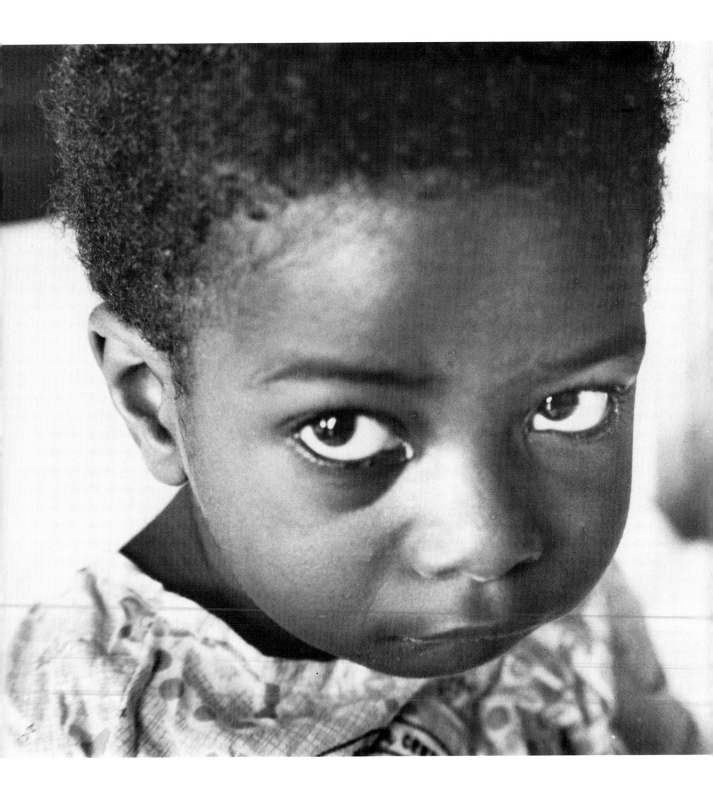

Being angry isn't the only feeling you may have. You may also feel scared. Many things about being in the hospital frighten people. The sight of patients who are much sicker than you may be upsetting or frightening. You may worry that you'll become like them or catch what they have. This won't happen, but it is a common fear.

Because you're scared you might also imagine the worst that can happen—that you'll be hurt in some unexpected way, or feel more pain than you can handle, or even that you'll die. Being scared in these ways is normal, and can help to prepare you for what you have to go through. Imagining the worst, you can say after it's over, "That wasn't as bad as I thought it would be!"

It's natural to feel scared when you're facing any new experience. Even now that you know something about going to the hospital, you may still feel scared. Perhaps you have questions that weren't answered in this book. Or you may have questions about things in the book that aren't clear to you, or frighten you.

Don't keep those questions inside. Ask your mother or father, or your doctor or nurse. If no one is around when you think of a question, write it down so you won't forget it. If you're worried, it's very important to try to understand what is going to happen to you.

So ask questions. And if you don't understand the answer you get, don't be afraid to ask again. People who work in hospitals sometimes answer quickly or use words that are hard to understand. Don't accept just any answer to your question—ask for an answer that is clear to you.

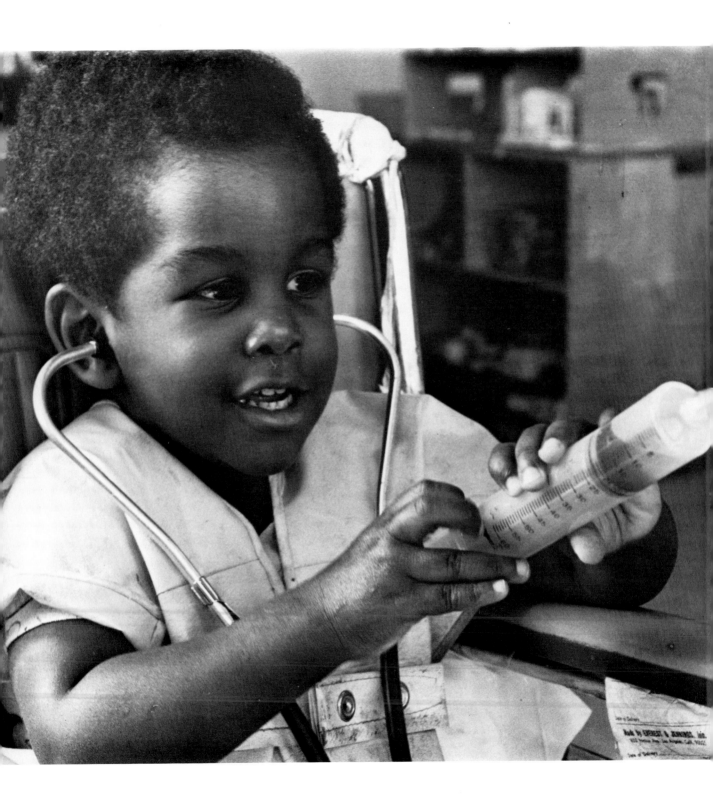

Sometimes people feel that they're in the hospital because they've done something wrong and are being punished. In fact, there is really no good reason why people get sick and have to go to the hospital. But to give it a reason, they sometimes think, "It must be something I did and now I'm being punished." That simply isn't true. Even if you did something you feel bad about, going to the hospital is not a punishment.

One thing you should not feel ashamed of is wetting your bed. That can happen to anyone who is nervous or upset. If you should wet the bed, the nurse will understand and will make your bed with a special sheet. No one will laugh at you or be angry. People in the hospital know that bed-wetting can happen there, even if it never happens at home.

Being alone and away from your own bed can make you feel sad. It's not easy to leave your home and your friends and go to a new place. So it might make you feel better to bring a favorite thing from home—a toy, a book or some snapshots of your family and friends. You might also bring a camera with you and take pictures during your hospital visit, so you can show your friends later what it was like.

Naturally, you'd be happier not being in the hospital. But while you're there, you may find things to enjoy. You may learn something about what doctors do, how your body works, and what kinds of problems other people have. You'll also learn something about yourself. You'll learn that you can get through a difficult experience.

When Am I Going Home?

~~~~~~~~~~~

You won't be kept in the hospital a day longer than is necessary. Everybody there understands how much you want to go home. And they understand, too, that home is where you should be.

Going to the hospital isn't easy, but as soon as the doctors feel you're well enough, you'll be home again.